Tell ME What YOU Remember

SPORT

Sarah Ridley

W
FRANKLIN WATTS
LONDON • SYDNEY

Franklin Watts
First published in Great Britain in 2015 by
The Watts Publishing Group

Series editor: Sarah Peutrill
Series design: Basement68

The Author and Publisher would
like to thank everyone who has
kindly contributed their photos
and memories to this book.

Dewey classification: 902
HB ISBN: 978 1 4451 4007 0
Library Ebook ISBN: 978 1 4451 4008 7

Printed in China

Franklin Watts
An imprint of
Hachette Children's Group
Part of The Watts Publishing Group
Carmelite House
50 Victoria Embankment
London EC4Y 0DZ

An Hachette UK Company
www.hachette.co.uk

www.franklinwatts.co.uk

Picture credits: Action Plus/
Alamy: 7b, 13. Action Plus/
Topfoto: 17b. AFP/Getty Images:
21b. © Laura Bosomworth: 19b.
BPEOSA/BPE Archive Image
Collection/MEPL: 8. Clive
Brunskill/Getty Images: 15b.
Colorsport: 20t. Bob Daemmrich/
Alamy: 22b. Fox Photos/Getty
Images: 14. John Gay/HIP/
Alamy: 12c. Henry Grant/MOL:
5, 11t, Keystone/Getty Images:
15t, 18b. Keystone/Hulton/Getty
Images: 21t. Kodak Collection/
SSPL: 4b. Eamonn McCabe/Getty
Images: 15c. Mondadori/Getty
Images: 20b. John Murray/Picture
Post/Getty Images: front cover
t, 9c. Popperfoto/Getty Images:
front cover b, 7t, 16, 18c, 19t.
Bob Thomas/Popperfoto/Getty
Images: 6. Topfoto: 4t. All other
photographs are kindly given
by the people who contributed
their memories.

Every attempt has been made
to clear copyright. Should there
be any inadvertent omission
please apply to the publisher
for rectification.

Contents

Playing the Game

Are you learning to swim? Do you like playing sport or watching it? Many of the rules of the sports we play today were written down over a hundred years ago. Other sports are much more recent.

Football and rugby became separate games when the rules were written down in the 1860s and 1870s. This team photo shows the England football team in 1892.

Britain used to govern lots of countries across its empire. When British people went to live in these countries, they took their sports with them.

A cricket match between England and Australia in Sydney, Australia in 1930.

Memories are what we remember about the past. Everyone has different memories about the sport they have played or watched over their lifetime. Talking to people about what they remember can help us to learn about the past.

Sarah, born 1963, remembers...

On sports day, everyone took part in races along a track marked out on the grass. There were winners and losers. As well as running races, we took part in three-legged races, sack races and wheelbarrow races. We won coloured ribbons fixed onto safety pins.

Women and Girls

In the past, sports were often divided into sports for women and girls, and sports for men and boys. Some doctors and other powerful people made decisions that kept women and girls out of certain sports for years.

The Dick, Kerr Ladies formed a factory football team during the First World War (1914–18). After the war, the Football Association banned women from playing on their grounds, probably because they did not like to see women playing a 'man's sport'.

1884 Women played tennis in the first Ladies' Championships at Wimbledon.

1921 Women's football teams were banned from playing on Football Association grounds (until 1971).

1982 The first international women's rugby match took place.

2012 Women finally took part in all Olympic sports.

Women first competed at the Olympic Games in 1900 but they were only allowed to take part in a few sports. The first women's 800 metres race took place at the 1928 Olympics. When some runners collapsed, the Olympic Committee decided that this event was too dangerous for women. In 1960 women were allowed to compete in the 800 metres again, which is when this photo was taken.

Kitty, born 1994, remembers...

The England team, wearing white, won the Women's Rugby World Cup in 2014.

At my school, we played netball, hockey, football, cricket, lacrosse and many other sports. Our warm-up exercise for rugby was rolling around on the muddy pitch. Some of us enjoyed it more than others!

Sport at School

By the 1930s most schoolchildren were taking part in some sort of school sport. It became easier for schools to teach sport properly when the government decided that all schools should have playing fields in 1944. Thousands of these sports fields were sold off during the 1980s and 1990s.

Barbara, born 1933, remembers...

In **1944**, all schools had to teach sport for the first time and playing fields were added to schools.
During the **1980s** and **1990s** many playing fields were sold for housing.
In **1997**, the government decided that all children should do at least two hours of school sport a week.

At primary school, we did exercises in lines, called drill, like these girls. I liked them because they were easy to follow and everyone was doing the same thing.

Bill, born 1937, remembers...

I won the junior sprint at sports day in the same year as the 1948 London Olympics. I also won the high jump and the long jump that year, after I'd practised endlessly in our garden.

Jane, born 1942, remembers...

At high school we played hockey in all weathers. Our skirts, like those worn by these girls in 1955, were made from masses of material that got in the way!

Lionel, born 1943, remembers...

I was in my school rugby team. As a treat, we were taken to Twickenham Stadium to watch a game.

I played lacrosse at school. We ran up and down the pitch, throwing and catching a rubber ball using the net on the end of our lacrosse sticks.

Jane, born 1963, remembers...

For part of our PE lessons at junior school we followed instructions from a BBC radio programme called Music and Movement. We balanced, stretched and moved to the music and sometimes acted out a scene.

Trevor, born 1970, remembers...

When I was growing up I loved playing sport. My favourites were hockey and cricket. I still play both sports. Hockey is a much faster game now because we play on AstroTurf rather than grass pitches.

These schoolboys were attending football coaching at school in 1980. Over the next 20 years, around 5,000 sports pitches and playing fields were sold off, so children had less places to play sport or be active. Many schoolchildren did not get the chance to play team sports any more.

Ben, born 1993, remembers...

There was not much space to play sport at my primary school but one day a hockey player came to show us the game. That year the school entered a team in a tournament. Only three of us knew the rules so we didn't do that well!

FIND OUT MORE

Ask your parents and grandparents about their memories of school sport. Which sports did they play and what did they wear to do sport?

11

Learning to Swim

Today most people learn to swim in indoor swimming pools at the local leisure centre. In the 1920s and 1930s many new open-air pools or lidos were built. Swimming became an incredibly popular sport and pastime.

Children were learning swimming strokes on the poolside when this photo was taken at the lido in Blackpool around 1950. This huge pool opened in 1923.

Jessie, born 1940, remembers...

My mum taught me to swim on family holidays at the seaside by standing in the sea and holding my chin up. Later on, at school, we had swimming lessons in the sea. The teacher sat in a rowing boat, shouting out instructions!

Liz, born 1979, remembers...

I learnt to swim at classes at school and by going swimming with my family. I had asthma but swimming helped to make my breathing stronger. I used to copy the strokes of swimmers on TV and was very proud when I was picked to swim at sports day.

Ellie Simmonds won four medals at the 2012 Paralympics. She joined her local swimming club at the age of five. When people noticed how quick she was, she received special training to help her improve.

London 2012
Paralympic Games

FIND OUT MORE

Compare swimsuits today with the one that Jessie is wearing on page 12.

13

Watching Sport

Before and after the Second World War (1939–45), crowds of people flocked to watch football or cricket matches, horse racing or motor sports. During the 1950s, as more people could afford to buy a television, many swopped to watching sport on TV.

Thousands of football fans stood together to watch matches at their local football ground every Saturday afternoon in the first half of the twentieth century. This photo was taken in 1948 at the FA Cup Final. Which teams were playing? How many women or girls can you spot?

IF YOU DON'T NEED IT - DON'T BUY IT -
Buy NATIONAL SAVINGS instead

MANCHESTER U^{TD}   BLACKPOOL

At this cricket test match between the West Indies and England in 1963, spectators celebrated when the West Indies won. Most of these people had recently moved from the West Indies to live in England.

Suzanne, born 1966, remembers...

In my family we all gathered around the TV each year to watch the Cambridge and Oxford boat crews battle it out. I didn't find it that interesting but I do remember watching the Cambridge boat sink in 1978.

Eliza, born 1999, remembers...

I like watching athletics and tennis. It was agony watching the end of the Murray Wimbledon final in 2013 and it was such a relief when he won.

FIND OUT MORE

Ask adults you know for their special sport memories.

Football

Football is the most popular sport in the world today. The Football Association wrote down the rules of the game in 1863. Football clubs sprang up in towns and villages, factories and schools. As many people have enjoyed watching football as playing it over the years.

1863 The Football Association established the rules of football.

1921 Women were banned from playing football on Football Association grounds.

1930 The first Football World Cup tournament was held in Uruguay.

1966 The World Cup was held in England and England won.

1971 The Football Association lifted the ban on women's football.

2002 Football became the top sport for women and girls to play.

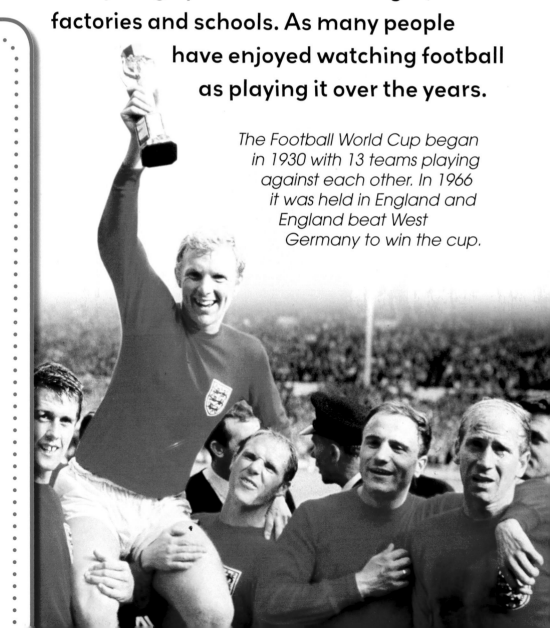

The Football World Cup began in 1930 with 13 teams playing against each other. In 1966 it was held in England and England beat West Germany to win the cup.

Irene, born 1939, remembers...

I went to my first Leicester City Football Club match in the 1950s. Everyone had to stand, packed closely together. In the 1990s I went again. There were seats for everyone and the floodlit pitch was magical.

Simon, born 1963, remembers...

I played football all the time when I was growing up — with my brothers, with friends, at school and in a Sunday league. My mother never worried about where I was. Every Saturday evening I watched *Match of the Day* on TV.

Hope Powell, in blue, was captain of Croydon women's team when they won the Football Association Women's Cup Final in 1996. She later became England's first full-time women's football coach.

FIND OUT MORE

Use the Internet and books to find out more about the 1966 World Cup.

17

Keeping Fit

During the 1930s and 1940s, the government and other groups encouraged people to get fit by joining exercise classes. This was followed by a craze for aerobics in the 1970s and 1980s. In the 1990s, private gyms and health clubs became popular.

These factory workers made parts for planes used in the Second World War and took part in exercise classes during their lunch hour in 1944.

In the 1950s, thousands of women turned on their radios to join in with Eileen Fowler's keep-fit exercises. She set up the Keep-Fit Association in 1956 and appeared in her own TV show.

Jogging became popular in the 1960s as a way for anyone to get fit. Some people took their hobby further. Almost 8,000 people ran in the first London Marathon in March 1981, shown left.

Julie, born 1962, remembers...

I started to go to aerobics classes when I began work in the mid-1980s. I wanted to get fit so I went to classes during my lunch break.

Laura, born 1998, remembers...

I do the Park Run as often as I can on Saturday mornings. Lots of runners take part each week. Triathlon is really popular in Yorkshire. I took part in the Brownlee Triathlon North in 2014. We had to swim through a lake which was full of goose poo!

Olympics and Paralympics

The first modern Olympic Games took place in 1896. Since then the Olympic Games have been held in London three times – in 1908, 1948 and 2012. The Paralympics started as an archery competition for wheelchair athletes in 1948 and have developed into a huge event.

The 1948 London Olympics opened on 29 July. No new stadiums were built as the United Kingdom was short of money after the Second World War.

Dutch athlete, Fanny Blankers-Koen, became world famous when she won four gold medals at the 1948 Olympics. She was already 30 and a mother of two children at this time.

In 1960, the first international Paralympics were held in Italy. This photo was taken of the Italian team in the Olympic Village. Four hundred disabled athletes from 23 countries took part in these games.

The Summer Olympic Games have been held every four years since 1896, except for during the two world wars.

1948 First Winter Olympics held.
Sixteen athletes who had been injured during the Second World War took part in the first Stoke Mandeville Games. This competition eventually developed into the Paralympics.

1960 The first international Paralympic Games were held in Rome, Italy.

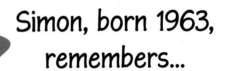

Simon, born 1963, remembers...

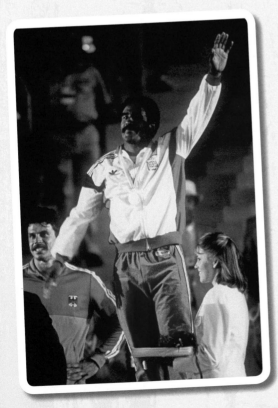

Daley Thompson was one of my sporting heroes. I thought he was Superman when he won the decathlon because he was so good in ten events. He looked so happy when he won gold medals for Britain at the 1980 and 1984 Olympics.

Eliza, born 1999, remembers...

I went to the London Olympics in 2012 with my cousins to watch some hockey matches. It was so exciting to walk around the Olympic Park, watch other events on the big screens and see the stadiums.

Ben, born 1993, remembers...

I watched a lot of the 2012 Paralympics events on TV. When David Weir said that beetroot juice had helped him to win the 800 metres wheelchair race, I started drinking it to see if it improved my running!

FIND OUT MORE

Why were the 1948 Olympics called the Austerity Olympics?

Timeline

Use this timeline to see at a glance some of the information in this book.

1863 The Football Association wrote down the rules of football.

1877 The All England Croquet and Lawn Tennis Club in Wimbledon held their first tennis championship.

1884 Women played each other at tennis in the first Ladies' Championships at Wimbledon.

1896 The first modern Olympic Games were held in Athens, Greece.

1920s/1930s Many open-air pools, called lidos, were built.

1921 The Football Association banned women's football teams from playing on FA grounds.

1928 Women ran the 800 metres race in the Olympics for the first time. They were not allowed to run it again until 1960.

1930 The first Football World Cup tournament was held.

1930s–1950s Thousands of people went to local football grounds to watch matches each weekend.

1944 The Education Act stated that sport must be taught in all schools.

1948 The Olympic Games were held in London. The first Stoke Mandeville Games held an archery contest between men and women who had become disabled during the Second World War.

1956 The Keep Fit Association was set up.

1960 The first International Paralympics were held in Rome, Italy.

1966 The Football World Cup was held in England.

1971 The Football Association lifted the ban preventing women's football teams from playing on their grounds.

1981 The first London Marathon was held. Women rugby players played their first international match.

1980s/1990s Many school playing fields were sold off to raise money.

1997 The British government decided that all schoolchildren must do at least two hours of sport per week.

2012 The Olympic Games were held in London. It was the first time that women took part in all Olympic sports.

2013 British tennis player, Andy Murray, won the Wimbledon Men's Final.

2014 The England Women's Rugby team won the World Cup.